This Maid Of Honor
GETS
SHIT
DONE!

THE ULTIMATE PLANNER

Belongs To:

_____

Master To-Do List

- [ ] _____
- [ ] _____
- [ ] _____
- [ ] _____
- [ ] _____
- [ ] _____
- [ ] _____
- [ ] _____
- [ ] _____
- [ ] _____
- [ ] _____
- [ ] _____
- [ ] _____
- [ ] _____
- [ ] _____
- [ ] _____
- [ ] _____

- [ ] _____
- [ ] _____
- [ ] _____
- [ ] _____
- [ ] _____
- [ ] _____
- [ ] _____
- [ ] _____
- [ ] _____
- [ ] _____
- [ ] _____
- [ ] _____
- [ ] _____
- [ ] _____
- [ ] _____
- [ ] _____
- [ ] _____

Master *To-Do List*

☐ _____

☐ _____

☐ _____

☐ _____

☐ _____

☐ _____

☐ _____

☐ _____

☐ _____

☐ _____

☐ _____

☐ _____

☐ _____

☐ _____

☐ _____

☐ _____

☐ _____

☐ _____

☐ _____

☐ _____

☐ _____

☐ _____

☐ _____

☐ _____

☐ _____

☐ _____

☐ _____

☐ _____

☐ _____

☐ _____

☐ _____

☐ _____

Important Dates At A Glance

Wedding Date _____

Save The Date Mailing By _____

Coordinate Gift Registry _____

Dress Shopping _____

Meeting With Caterer _____

Invitations Mailed By _____

Bridal Shower _____

Final Dress Alterations _____

Finalize Guest List _____

Bachelorette Party _____

Wedding Day Hair/Nails _____

Vendor Contact List

WEDDING CAKE

Vendor:

Contact:

Email:

Phone:

Notes:

CEREMONY VENUE

Vendor:

Contact:

Email:

Phone:

Notes:

RECEPTION ENTERTAINMENT

Vendor:

Contact:

Email:

Phone:

Notes:

RECEPTION VENUE

Vendor:

Contact:

Email:

Phone:

Notes:

Vendor Contact List

BACHELORETTE PARTY VENUE

Vendor:

Contact:

Email:

Phone:

Notes:

WEDDING HAIR

Vendor:

Contact:

Email:

Phone:

Notes:

WEDDING NAILS

Vendor:

Contact:

Email:

Phone:

Notes:

CEREMONY OFFICIANT

Vendor:

Contact:

Email:

Phone:

Notes:

Vendor Contact List

FLORIST

Vendor:

Contact:

Email:

Phone:

Notes:

CATERER

Vendor:

Contact:

Email:

Phone:

Notes:

EM CEE

Vendor:

Contact:

Email:

Phone:

Notes:

LIMO/TRANSPORTATION

Vendor:

Contact:

Email:

Phone:

Notes:

Vendor Contact List

WEDDING COORDINATOR

Vendor:

Contact:

Email:

Phone:

Notes:

PHOTOGRAPHER

Vendor:

Contact:

Email:

Phone:

Notes:

VIDEOGRAPHER

Vendor:

Contact:

Email:

Phone:

Notes:

ALTERATIONS

Vendor:

Contact:

Email:

Phone:

Notes:

Vendor Contact List

Vendor:

Contact:

Email:

Phone:

Notes:

Vendor:

Contact:

Email:

Phone:

Notes:

Vendor:

Contact:

Email:

Phone:

Notes:

Vendor:

Contact:

Email:

Phone:

Notes:

Vendor Contact List

Vendor:

Contact:

Email:

Phone:

Notes:

Vendor:

Contact:

Email:

Phone:

Notes:

Vendor:

Contact:

Email:

Phone:

Notes:

Vendor:

Contact:

Email:

Phone:

Notes:

Monthly *Planner*

Month Of:_____

SUN	MON	TUES	WED	THURS	FRI	SAT

Monthly *Planner*

Month Of:_____

SUN	MON	TUES	WED	THURS	FRI	SAT

Monthly *Planner*

Month Of: _____

SUN	MON	TUES	WED	THURS	FRI	SAT

Monthly *Planner*

Month Of:_____

SUN	MON	TUES	WED	THURS	FRI	SAT

Monthly *Planner*

Month Of:_____

SUN	MON	TUES	WED	THURS	FRI	SAT

Monthly *Planner*

Month Of:_____

SUN	MON	TUES	WED	THURS	FRI	SAT

Monthly *Planner*

Month Of:_____

SUN	MON	TUES	WED	THURS	FRI	SAT

Weekly Planner

Sunday

Week Of: _____

Monday

To Do List:

- ☐ _____
- ☐ _____
- ☐ _____
- ☐ _____
- ☐

Tuesday

Wednesday

APPOINTMENTS

Date	Time	Vendor	Contact Info

Thursday

Friday

Notes

Saturday

Weekly Planner

Sunday	Week Of: _____

To Do List:

- ☐ _____
- ☐ _____
- ☐ _____
- ☐ _____
- ☐ _____

Monday

Tuesday

Wednesday

APPOINTMENTS

Date	Time	Vendor	Contact Info

Thursday

Friday

Notes

Saturday

Weekly Planner

Sunday

Monday

Tuesday

Wednesday

Thursday

Friday

Saturday

Week Of:_____

To Do List:

- ☐
- ☐
- ☐
- ☐
- ☐

APPOINTMENTS

Date	Time	Vendor	Contact Info

Notes

Weekly *Planner*

Sunday

Monday

Tuesday

Wednesday

Thursday

Friday

Saturday

Week Of:_____

To Do List:

- ☐
- ☐
- ☐
- ☐
- ☐

APPOINTMENTS

Date	Time	Vendor	Contact Info

Notes

Weekly Planner

Sunday

Monday

Tuesday

Wednesday

Thursday

Friday

Saturday

Week Of:_____

To Do List:

- ☐
- ☐
- ☐
- ☐
- ☐

APPOINTMENTS

Date	Time	Vendor	Contact Info

Notes

Monthly *Planner*

Month Of:_____

SUN	MON	TUES	WED	THURS	FRI	SAT

Weekly *Planner*

| Sunday | Week Of:_____ |

Sunday

Monday

Tuesday

Wednesday

Thursday

Friday

Saturday

To Do List:

☐

☐

☐

☐

☐

APPOINTMENTS

Date	Time	Vendor	Contact Info

Notes

Weekly Planner

| Sunday | Week Of: _____ |

Sunday

Monday

Tuesday

Wednesday

Thursday

Friday

Saturday

To Do List:

- ☐
- ☐
- ☐
- ☐
- ☐

APPOINTMENTS

Date	Time	Vendor	Contact Info

Notes

Weekly *Planner*

Sunday

Monday

Tuesday

Wednesday

Thursday

Friday

Saturday

Week Of:_____

To Do List:

- ☐
- ☐
- ☐
- ☐
- ☐

APPOINTMENTS

Date	Time	Vendor	Contact Info

Notes

Weekly *Planner*

Sunday

Monday

Tuesday

Wednesday

Thursday

Friday

Saturday

Week Of:_____

To Do List:

- ☐ _____
- ☐ _____
- ☐ _____
- ☐ _____
- ☐ _____

APPOINTMENTS

Date	Time	Vendor	Contact Info

Notes

Weekly Planner

Sunday	

Week Of: _____

Monday	

To Do List:

- ☐ _____
- ☐ _____
- ☐ _____
- ☐ _____
- ☐ _____

Tuesday	

Wednesday	

APPOINTMENTS

Date	Time	Vendor	Contact Info

Thursday	

Friday	

Notes

Saturday	

Monthly *Planner*

Month Of:_____

SUN	MON	TUES	WED	THURS	FRI	SAT

Weekly Planner

Sunday

Monday

Tuesday

Wednesday

Thursday

Friday

Saturday

Week Of:_____

To Do List:

- [ ]
- [ ]
- [ ]
- [ ]
- [ ]

APPOINTMENTS			
Date	Time	Vendor	Contact Info

Notes

Weekly Planner

Sunday

Monday

Tuesday

Wednesday

Thursday

Friday

Saturday

Week Of:_____

To Do List:

- [ ] _____
- [ ] _____
- [ ] _____
- [ ] _____
- [ ] _____

APPOINTMENTS

Date	Time	Vendor	Contact Info

Notes

Weekly Planner

Sunday	Week Of: _____

Sunday

Monday

Tuesday

Wednesday

Thursday

Friday

Saturday

To Do List:

☐ _____
☐ _____
☐ _____
☐ _____
☐ _____

APPOINTMENTS

Date	Time	Vendor	Contact Info

Notes

Weekly Planner

Sunday

Monday

Tuesday

Wednesday

Thursday

Friday

Saturday

Week Of: _____

To Do List:

☐ _____

☐ _____

☐ _____

☐ _____

☐ _____

APPOINTMENTS

Date	Time	Vendor	Contact Info

Notes

Weekly Planner

| Sunday | Week Of: _____ |

Sunday

Monday

Tuesday

Wednesday

Thursday

Friday

Saturday

To Do List:

☐
☐
☐
☐
☐

APPOINTMENTS

Date	Time	Vendor	Contact Info

Notes

Monthly *Planner*

Month Of:_____

SUN	MON	TUES	WED	THURS	FRI	SAT

Weekly Planner

| Sunday | Week Of: _____ |

Sunday

Monday

Tuesday

Wednesday

Thursday

Friday

Saturday

To Do List:

- ☐
- ☐
- ☐
- ☐
- ☐

APPOINTMENTS

Date	Time	Vendor	Contact Info

Notes

Weekly Planner

Sunday
Monday
Tuesday
Wednesday
Thursday
Friday
Saturday

Week Of: _____

To Do List:

- ☐
- ☐
- ☐
- ☐
- ☐

APPOINTMENTS

Date	Time	Vendor	Contact Info

Notes

Weekly Planner

Sunday

Monday

Tuesday

Wednesday

Thursday

Friday

Saturday

Week Of:_____

To Do List:

- ☐
- ☐
- ☐
- ☐
- ☐

APPOINTMENTS

Date	Time	Vendor	Contact Info

Notes

Weekly $Planner$

Sunday

Monday

Tuesday

Wednesday

Thursday

Friday

Saturday

Week Of: _____

To Do List:

☐ _____
☐ _____
☐ _____
☐ _____
☐ _____

APPOINTMENTS

Date	Time	Vendor	Contact Info

Notes

Weekly Planner

| Sunday | Week Of:_____ |

Sunday

Monday

Tuesday

Wednesday

Thursday

Friday

Saturday

To Do List:

☐ _____
☐ _____
☐ _____
☐ _____
☐

APPOINTMENTS

Date	Time	Vendor	Contact Info

Notes

Monthly *Planner*

Month Of:_____

SUN	MON	TUES	WED	THURS	FRI	SAT

Weekly _Planner_

Sunday

Monday

Tuesday

Wednesday

Thursday

Friday

Saturday

Week Of:_____

To Do List:

- ☐
- ☐
- ☐
- ☐
- ☐

APPOINTMENTS

Date	Time	Vendor	Contact Info

Notes

Weekly *Planner*

Sunday

Monday

Tuesday

Wednesday

Thursday

Friday

Saturday

Week Of:_____

To Do List:

- [ ]
- [ ]
- [ ]
- [ ]
- [ ]

APPOINTMENTS

Date	Time	Vendor	Contact Info

Notes

Weekly *Planner*

Sunday	Week Of: _____
	To Do List:
Monday	☐ _____
	☐ _____
Tuesday	☐ _____
	☐ _____
Wednesday	☐ _____

Sunday
Monday
Tuesday
Wednesday
Thursday
Friday
Saturday

Week Of: _____

To Do List:

- ☐
- ☐
- ☐
- ☐
- ☐

APPOINTMENTS

Date	Time	Vendor	Contact Info

Notes

Weekly _Planner_

Sunday

Monday

Tuesday

Wednesday

Thursday

Friday

Saturday

Week Of:_____

To Do List:

- [ ]
- [ ]
- [ ]
- [ ]
- [ ]

APPOINTMENTS

Date	Time	Vendor	Contact Info

Notes

Weekly Planner

Sunday

Monday

Tuesday

Wednesday

Thursday

Friday

Saturday

Week Of:_____

To Do List:

☐	
☐	
☐	
☐	
☐	

APPOINTMENTS

Date	Time	Vendor	Contact Info

Notes

Monthly *Planner*

Month Of:_____

SUN	MON	TUES	WED	THURS	FRI	SAT

Weekly Planner

Sunday

Monday

Tuesday

Wednesday

Thursday

Friday

Saturday

Week Of:_____

To Do List:

- ☐
- ☐
- ☐
- ☐
- ☐

APPOINTMENTS

Date	Time	Vendor	Contact Info

Notes

Weekly Planner

Sunday

Monday

Tuesday

Wednesday

Thursday

Friday

Saturday

Week Of:_____

To Do List:

- ☐
- ☐
- ☐
- ☐
- ☐

APPOINTMENTS

Date	Time	Vendor	Contact Info

Notes

Weekly *Planner*

Sunday

Monday

Tuesday

Wednesday

Thursday

Friday

Saturday

Week Of:_____

To Do List:

- ☐ _____
- ☐ _____
- ☐ _____
- ☐ _____
- ☐

APPOINTMENTS

Date	Time	Vendor	Contact Info

Notes

Weekly *Planner*

Sunday

Monday

Tuesday

Wednesday

Thursday

Friday

Saturday

Week Of:_____

To Do List:

☐ _____

☐ _____

☐ _____

☐ _____

☐ _____

APPOINTMENTS

Date	Time	Vendor	Contact Info

Notes

Weekly Planner

Sunday

Monday

Tuesday

Wednesday

Thursday

Friday

Saturday

Week Of:_____

To Do List:

- [ ]
- [ ]
- [ ]
- [ ]
- [ ]

APPOINTMENTS

Date	Time	Vendor	Contact Info

Notes

1 Week Before

	THINGS TO DO:	NOTES:
MONDAY		
TUESDAY		
WEDNESDAY		
THURSDAY		

REMINDERS & NOTES:

1 Week Before

	THINGS TO DO:	NOTES:
FRIDAY		
SATURDAY		
SUNDAY		

LEFT TO DO:

REMINDERS:

NOTES:

Wedding Planner

- PLANNING GUIDELINE -

- ☐ ATTEND REHEARSAL DINNER
- ☐ FINISH HONEYMOON PACKING
- ☐ GREET OUT OF TOWN GUESTS

- ☐ GET MANICURE/PEDICURE
- ☐ CHECK ON WEDDING VENUE
- ☐ CHECK WEATHER TO PREPARE

- ☐ GIVE GIFTS TO WEDDING PARTY
- ☐ CONFIRM RINGS FIT
- ☐ GET A GOOD NIGHT'S SLEEP

Things To Do	Status

TOP PRIORITIES

NOTES & IDEAS

APPOINTMENTS & REMINDERS

THINGS TO REMEMBER FOR TOMORROW:

The Big Day!

(reminders for the Maid Of Honor and The Bride)

☐ GET HAIR & MAKE UP DONE

☐ HAVE A HEALTHY BREAKFAST

☐ ENJOY YOUR BIG DAY!

☐ MEET WITH BRIDESMAIDS

☐ GIVE RINGS TO BEST MAN

TO DO LIST:

Bridal Shower Budget

Total Budget

CATEGORY	BUDGET	ACTUAL COST	DEPOSIT PAID	BALANCE	DUE
INVITATIONS					
Save The Date					
Invitations					
Envelopes					
Thank You Cards					
Postage					
VENUE					
Rental Fee					
Misc.					
FOOD & DRINK					
Catering					
Beverages					
Alcoholic					
Non-alcoholic					
Cake					
Plates/Bowls					
Utensils					
Napkins					

Bridal Shower Budget

CATEGORY	BUDGET	ACTUAL COST	DEPOSIT PAID	BALANCE	DUE
DECORATIONS					
Table Decorations					
Venue Decorations					
Signs, Banners, Wall Decor					
Misc. Decorations					
FAVORS & GAMES					
Games					
Prizes					
Favors					
ENTERTAINMENT					
OTHER					

Bridal Shower Planner

PARTY DETAILS
DATE
TIME
VENUE
THEME
NOTES

GAMES/ACTIVITIES

Food/Drink

Decorations

GUEST LIST		
NAME	CONTACT INFO	RSVP

GUEST LIST

NAME	CONTACT INFO	RSVP

Shopping List

- [ ] _____
- [ ] _____
- [ ] _____
- [ ] _____
- [ ] _____
- [ ] _____
- [ ] _____
- [ ] _____
- [ ] _____
- [ ] _____
- [ ] _____
- [ ] _____
- [ ] _____
- [ ] _____
- [ ] _____
- [ ] _____

- [ ] _____
- [ ] _____
- [ ] _____
- [ ] _____
- [ ] _____
- [ ] _____
- [ ] _____
- [ ] _____
- [ ] _____
- [ ] _____
- [ ] _____
- [ ] _____
- [ ] _____
- [ ] _____
- [ ] _____
- [ ] _____

Bachelorette Party Budget

Total Budget

CATEGORY	BUDGET	ACTUAL COST	DEPOSIT PAID	BALANCE	DUE
INVITATIONS					
Save The Date					
Invitations					
Envelopes					
Thank You Cards					
Postage					
VENUE					
Rental Fee					
Misc.					
FOOD & DRINK					
Catering					
Beverages					
Alcoholic					
Non-alcoholic					
Cake					
Plates/Bowls					
Utensils					
Napkins					

Bachelorette Party Budget

CATEGORY	BUDGET	ACTUAL COST	DEPOSIT PAID	BALANCE	DUE
DECORATIONS					
Table Decorations					
Venue Decorations					
Signs, Banners, Wall Decor					
Misc. Decorations					
FAVORS & GAMES					
Games					
Prizes					
Favors					
ENTERTAINMENT					
OTHER					

Bachelorette Party Planner

PARTY DETAILS
DATE
TIME
VENUE
THEME
NOTES

GAMES/ACTIVITIES

Food/Drink

Decorations

NAME	CONTACT INFO	RSVP

GUEST LIST		
NAME	CONTACT INFO	RSVP

Shopping List

- [ ] _____
- [ ] _____
- [ ] _____
- [ ] _____
- [ ] _____
- [ ] _____
- [ ] _____
- [ ] _____
- [ ] _____
- [ ] _____
- [ ] _____
- [ ] _____
- [ ] _____
- [ ] _____
- [ ] _____
- [ ] _____

- [ ] _____
- [ ] _____
- [ ] _____
- [ ] _____
- [ ] _____
- [ ] _____
- [ ] _____
- [ ] _____
- [ ] _____
- [ ] _____
- [ ] _____
- [ ] _____
- [ ] _____
- [ ] _____
- [ ] _____
- [ ] _____

Wedding Day Emergency Kit

Apparel Repair Kit

- [ ] Small Scissors
- [ ] Safety Pins
- [ ] Hem Tape
- [ ] Clear Nail Polish
- [ ] Tide-To-Go
- [ ] Lint Roller
- [ ] Sewing Kit

Hair

- [ ] Comb/Brush
- [ ] Bobby Pins
- [ ] Hair Ties
- [ ] Hairspray
- [ ] Dry Shampoo
- [ ] Hair Straightener/Curling Iron

Toiletries

- [ ] Q-Tips
- [ ] Tweezers
- [ ] Nail File
- [ ] Touch-up Nail Polish
- [ ] Deodorant
- [ ] Perfume
- [ ] Tissues
- [ ] Tampons/Pads
- [ ] Toothbrush/Paste/Floss
- [ ] Lotion

Meds/First Aid

- [ ] Antacid
- [ ] Band-Aids
- [ ] Tylenol/Motrin
- [ ] Contact Solution
- [ ] Allergy Medicine
- [ ] Bug Spray

Ideas/Draft Maid Of Honor Speech

Ideas/Draft Maid Of Honor Speech

Notes/Ideas/Memories

Notes/Ideas/Memories

Notes/Ideas/Memories

Notes/Ideas/Memories

Notes/Ideas/Memories

Notes/Ideas/Memories

Notes/Ideas/Memories

Notes/Ideas/Memories

Notes/Ideas/Memories

Notes/Ideas/Memories

Notes/Ideas/Memories

Notes/Ideas/Memories

Notes/Ideas/Memories

Notes/Ideas/Memories

Notes/Ideas/Memories

Notes/Ideas/Memories

Notes/Ideas/Memories

Notes/Ideas/Memories

Notes/Ideas/Memories

Notes/Ideas/Memories

Notes/Ideas/Memories

Notes/Ideas/Memories

Notes/Ideas/Memories

Notes/Ideas/Memories

Notes/Ideas/Memories

Notes/Ideas/Memories

Notes/Ideas/Memories

Notes/Ideas/Memories

Notes/Ideas/Memories

Notes/Ideas/Memories

Notes/Ideas/Memories

Notes/Ideas/Memories

Notes/Ideas/Memories

Notes/Ideas/Memories

Notes/Ideas/Memories

Notes/Ideas/Memories

Notes/Ideas/Memories

Notes/Ideas/Memories

Notes/Ideas/Memories

Notes/Ideas/Memories

Notes/Ideas/Memories

Notes/Ideas/Memories

Notes/Ideas/Memories

Notes/Ideas/Memories

Notes/Ideas/Memories

Notes/Ideas/Memories

Notes/Ideas/Memories

Notes/Ideas/Memories

Notes/Ideas/Memories

Notes/Ideas/Memories

Notes/Ideas/Memories

Notes/Ideas/Memories

Notes/Ideas/Memories

Notes/Ideas/Memories

Notes/Ideas/Memories

Notes/Ideas/Memories

Notes/Ideas/Memories

Made in the USA
San Bernardino,
CA